in ▪ thē ▪ sun

SRA
McGraw-Hill
*Columbus, Ohio*

*A Division of The* ***McGraw·Hill*** *Companies*

Written by
Siegfried Englemann
Elaine C. Bruner

Illustrated by
Jan Pyk

**www.sra4kids.com**

***SRA/McGraw-Hill***
*A Division of The* ***McGraw-Hill*** *Companies*



Printed in the United States of America.

Send all inquiries to:
SRA/McGraw-Hill
8787 Orion Place
Columbus, OH 43240-4027

ISBN 0-02-674871-1

22 23 24 25 26 QST 11 10 09 08

a ■ man ■ had ■ a ■ ram.

that ■ ram ■ sat ■ in ■ thē ■ sun.

a ■ rat ■ sat ■ in ■ thē ■ sun.

thē ▪ ram ▪ and ▪ thē ▪ rat ▪

had ▪ fun.